Introducing
Ephesians

Introducing Ephesians

A Book for Today

SIMON AUSTEN

Series Editor: Adrian Reynolds

PTRESOURCES

CHRISTIAN
FOCUS

Copyright © Simon Austen 2012

ISBN 978-1-78191-059-7

First published in 2012 as the introduction to
Teaching Ephesians (ISBN 978-1-84550-684-1)
Published as a stand-alone title
in 2012
by
Christian Focus Publications,
Geanies House, Fearn,
Ross-shire, IV20 1TW, Scotland.
with
Proclamation Trust Resources,
Willcox House, 140-148 Borough High Street,
London, SE1 1LB, England, Great Britain.
www.proctrust.org.uk

www.christianfocus.com

Cover design by Daniel van Straaten
Printed by Bell and Bain

CONTENTS

Editor's Preface

Ephesians is one of the richest books of the New Testament, if not the Bible. In just six short chapters, the apostle Paul outlines God's plan for humanity and history and how that plan works itself out in the Christian life we live together. It's impossible to read Ephesians and not be moved by the greatness of God's purposes and the wonderful way he draws men and women from all backgrounds together in the church, the radiant church for which his Son, Christ Jesus, gave his life.

Reading Ephesians well will teach us about God, his salvation that he has made possible through his Son Jesus, the work of the Spirit in making us like Christ, the place and role of the church in history, the battle that Christians fight in and much more besides.

It's a good letter therefore for Christians to read on their own. But it's even better for Christians to read together, as *churches* (that was probably Paul's original intention). Paul's emphasis on what we are in Christ *as his people* (and not just as individuals) is very strong and even in this short introduction our author and guide, Simon Austen, explains that very well indeed.

This little volume is a brief introduction to the book, written by Simon, a church minister in the north of England.

Originally, these three chapters started life as part of Simon's contribution to our 'Teaching...' series. This series is written especially *for* Bible preachers and teachers *by* Bible preachers and teachers. They are more detailed than a devotional book, though not a full commentary; each volume is written to encourage those who have the serious responsibility of teaching God's Word in any context, especially through preaching. Each, therefore, contains analysis of what the passage means, matched together with how it may be taught and applied.

In this excerpt, Simon helps us get to grips with the book. Firstly, he does that by giving us some important Bible background. In the first chapter you'll learn a little more about Ephesus and the situation there. In the second, Simon guides us through some of the key themes of Ephesians, so you are helped to see what it is all about and what to look out for as you read the Bible text. In the third, we have included an edited version of chapter 1 of Simon's longer book – it is based on the first fourteen verses of Ephesians and serves as an excellent introduction to many of the themes.

I have edited these three chapters to provide you with a general introduction to the book. Like a traveller who steps off a plane or train at an unfamiliar destination and needs a moment to gather his or her bearings, this short book is designed to help you get your bearings in the book of Ephesians.

In reading it, I sincerely hope and pray that your enthusiasm for Ephesians will be kindled and that you will come to see that Ephesians is not just as a collection of well-known verses (saved by grace, marriage advice, the armour of God and so on). It is a rich feast, drawing back the curtain on God's plan for his people and how Christians together are both *in* Christ and called to be *like* Christ.

Perhaps you have been given this little book as part of a Bible study series or preaching series at church. Then, I hope it both introduces Ephesians well and gives you enthusiasm for what lies ahead. Perhaps you have simply picked it up and thought, 'Yes, I'd like to know a bit more about Ephesians.' I trust your prayer will be answered. If you enjoy it, as I trust you will, why not buy the full volume, *Teaching Ephesians*, particularly if you are in any kind of Bible teaching ministry in the church?

About The Proclamation Trust

The Proclamation Trust is a UK based charity that serves churches by championing the cause of Bible preaching and teaching. Our aim is to equip and encourage faithful Bible preachers and teachers wherever they may be found, but particularly in the UK. We do that through our training course (The Cornhill Training Course) and through conferences, online resources and books.

Our 'Teaching…' series is a key part of that work and there are currently 11 volumes in the series.

We believe that the Bible is God's written Word and that, by the work of the Holy Spirit, as it is faithfully preached God's voice is truly heard. The call of every Bible teacher is therefore to cast himself fully upon God and, in the words of the Apostle Paul to young Pastor Timothy, to 'correctly handle the word of truth' (2 Tim. 2:15). Many resources, including our podcast for preachers, are available from our website, www.proctrust.org.uk, where you can also read more about our work and ministry.

Adrian Reynolds
Series Editor, London, March 2012

I

Introducing Ephesians

For most of us our experience of church is mixed. It is a great privilege and delight to be a part of God's new community, to know that sense of love and acceptance and forgiveness; it is wonderful when we experience that quality of life and love which can only come from the regenerating work of the Spirit. But churches can also be very difficult. People fall out with one another, cliques form, powerful individuals hold sway, pastors are criticised. There is all too often a large gulf between what we are in Christ and what we are in reality. The result of this is that as the main distinguishing mark of being a disciple is destroyed (love for one another), so the main responsibilities of the church are diminished (evangelism, prayer and nurture). It can be very difficult for us to be what we know we are in Christ.

Ephesians is a letter for the church, a timeless exposition about becoming what we are in Christ. It sets forth the objective reality for all who are recipients of God's unmerited love and who have been made alive in Christ; and then it tells us how we might become what we are. Reading and understanding Ephesians is like being taken through the theological equivalent of a photographer's dark room. In the days before digital photography the picture was captured at the moment the camera's shutter opened, permanently set into the film, yet it still had to be developed. There, in the dark room, the picture slowly emerged; that which had been taken became a permanent reality for all to see.

In the same way we have been made alive and raised with Christ. As a result we have every spiritual blessing in him. The picture has been taken; but now the film must be developed, so that we can become what we are. Ephesians takes us on that journey, explaining the nature of the picture that has been taken and how the photograph can be developed, so that those who are God's people might become what they have been made in Christ.

It is a letter which has generated rich emotion, being described by one commentator as 'one of the most significant documents ever written.' It has been said by another that it matches Romans 'as a candidate for exercising the most influence on Christian thought and spirituality.' And yet it is a letter which many Christians know only in part. Its rich treasure for Christian thought and spirituality, and particularly its wonderfully developed teaching about the church, remains relatively untapped. We need to hear the message of this letter. We need to be challenged about our consumerist and individualistic views of salvation and of our relationship to the people to whom we have been joined together and of whom we are a part. And perhaps above all, we need to recapture the glorious reality of the local church as a beacon of the future and a picture of God's purposes in the world. The local church is not only the hope of the world; it also shows us where history is heading.

WELCOME TO EPHESUS!

The city of Ephesus, although once a Greek colony, had become by Paul's day the capital city of Roman Proconsular Asia. Powerful and cosmopolitan, it hosted the headquarters of the cult of Artemis (Diana), whose temple, which was rebuilt after being destroyed in the 4th century B.C., was now considered to be one of the seven wonders of the ancient world. Sitting in the Amphitheatre today and looking out to the now silted-up port, it is easy to imagine the once-thriving commercial centre and the relatively low-profile arrival of Paul and his companions as he travelled from Corinth back towards Jerusalem on his second missionary journey expedition. His three-year ministry (52-55 A.D., see Acts 20:31) influenced all of Asia and left us with a treasure-trove of Biblical encouragement and warning.

Luke's account of Paul's Ephesian ministry dominates Acts 19 and 20. Initially Paul entered the synagogue, speaking boldly there for three months and arguing persuasively about the Kingdom of

God. It is reasonable to assume that some of the Jews believed, not least because the letter he later wrote has so much to say about the relationship between Jew and Gentile but also because, when the opposition arose, Luke tells us that *some of them* became obstinate and refused to believe', (italics mine). Those who refused to respond 'publicly maligned the way'. (Acts 19:9). Others, presumably, didn't.

Those who had believed and were responding to the teaching moved with Paul to the lecture hall of Tyrannus, where he began a series of daily discussions which lasted for two years. As a result, 'All the Jews and Greeks who lived in the Province of Asia heard the word of the Lord.' (Acts 19:10). The letter to the Ephesians, written perhaps some six to eight years later (59-61 A.D.), would have been to all those in the region who responded to the word of God, a group which extended beyond the bounds of the city of Ephesus.

Luke tells us that Paul's ministry was associated with extraordinary miracles, perhaps a step above the usual apostolic expectation (2 Cor. 12:12). It may have been the particular adherence of some to the cult of the day which necessitated greater displays of divine power. Certainly it seems possible that some professed faith before being confronted with the real power of the gospel: following the experience of the seven sons of Sceva, who sought to invoke the name of Jesus in an attempt to exorcise, many of those who believed 'now came and openly confessed their evil deeds.' (Acts 19:18). Presumably prior to this incident they had 'believed' without experiencing the power of the gospel or the need to repent.

As Paul prepared to leave Ephesus, Luke provides us with an account of the city-wide riot instigated by Demetrius the silversmith. He had become aware that the gospel was taking root and that Paul had 'led astray large numbers of people here in Ephesus and in practically the whole province of Asia.' (Acts 19:26). The uproar which followed was marked by great confusion (some people did not even know why they were there; Acts 19:32) and perhaps just as much anti-Jewish as anti-Christian sentiment (as was seen by their response to Alexander the Jew). The fact that the officials protected Paul and the city clerk brought peace to the situation suggests that Luke's purpose in recounting this incident (in the words of John Stott) was 'clearly apologetic or political. He wanted to show that Rome had no case against Christianity in particular or Paul in general.'

What is clear from the book of Acts is that by the time Paul left, everyone in Ephesus and the wider province of Asia

had heard the gospel and many people, both Jews and Greeks, had believed.
Churches had been planted and leaders
had been appointed, so much so that when
we next hear about Paul and the church in
Ephesus, it is in the context of his exhor-
tation to the Ephesian elders.

AT THE ELDERS' MEETING
About a year has passed since Paul left
Ephesus and now he arrives down the
coast at Miletus, from where he summons
the Ephesian elders. Acts 20:25-35 is the
only speech in Acts directly to a Christian
audience and overwhelmingly it concerns
the health of the church in the region.
The leaders must watch themselves and
the flock of which the Holy Spirit has
made them overseers. Negatively, they
must be on their guard from false teachers who will emerge even from their own
number. Positively, they must hold on to
God and the word of his grace, which

can build them up and give them an inheritance among those who are sanctified (Acts 20:30-32).

After Paul's departure the church in Ephesus has a mixed history. He later encourages Timothy to stay in Ephesus in order that he may 'command certain men not to teach false doctrines any longer' (1 Tim. 1:3), concerned as he is that people may know how to conduct themselves in God's household, the pillar and foundation of the truth. (1 Tim. 3:15). It must have been extremely painful for Paul to see what happened to this fledgling church. As he writes his second letter to Timothy, revealing something more of the challenge for all churches in the last days, he reminds us that 'everyone in the Province of Asia has deserted me ... at my first defence no-one came to my support' (2 Tim. 1:15; 4:16).

Clearly the warnings of Acts 20 were needed and to a certain extent they were heeded. By the time we get to the book of Revelation the words of the risen Lord Jesus to the church in Ephesus suggest that the church was doctrinally pure and discerning; but now their problem had changed. They had lost their first love, they had failed to do the things they did at first; their evangelistic heart had gone cold.

As we survey the New Testament to see what happened to the church in Ephesus and in the province of Asia it makes for sobering reading. The gospel went out, faithfully proclaimed through patient daily ministry, so that all in the province of Asia heard the word of the Lord. Jews and Gentiles became Christians; pastor-teachers were appointed and charged to keep teaching and keep watch. Their tears of friendship and concern for Paul gave no indication that things would ever change, except that is, for Paul's solemn warning ... 'even from your own number men will arise and distort the truth in order to draw away disciples after them' (Acts 20:30). Later Timothy had to be left in the region to command such teachers to keep quiet. The church prevailed but lost her first love; and today the church in Ephesus is no more.

Paul's letter picks up all these concerns – the gospel, the need for teaching, the interaction of Christians with one another and the church with the world – and he reminds us of the spiritual warfare in which we are involved, not only as people become part of the church, but as we seek to remain as the church. We have much to learn.

Beyond the city

In the light of Paul's experience in Asia Minor, his letter to the Ephesians may well have been designed to be circulated around the churches in Western Asia Minor, centred around the busy city of

Ephesus with its population of 250,000. Paul clearly knew at least some of those to whom he was writing (1:16 and 6:19-20) whilst at the same time he may well have written it with others in mind (see 3:2; 4:21), desiring all Christians to understand the significance of what it meant to be part of God's new community.

The far-reaching implications and universal importance of understanding this truth make it difficult to suggest a particular 'occasion' which generated the letter. Inevitably many suggestions have been made, but perhaps in God's goodness the lack of an obvious setting enables the church of every generation to identify and benefit from these timeless truths. The only 'controversy' or difficulty we discover is the relationship between Jew and Gentile before coming to Christ, and the relationship of the church with the world after people have come to Christ. Such concerns need not be generated by particular historical situations but remain battles and challenges for all God's people, even if the nature of the barriers and difficulties may have changed with time.

2

Understanding
Ephesians:
in Christ

We must always hesitate to use a single verse to sum up a letter when the author chose to use many more words to convey his message. When we consider that the letter would probably have been read at one sitting to a gathered congregation (of all ages), it seems rather presumptuous to assume we can encapsulate the entire message in one sentence.

At the same time it is quite possible to trace themes in this letter, all of which ultimately relate to who we are in Christ. It is in him that we have every spiritual blessing; in him we have been chosen and raised – and through him we have been made into that one new entity, the church. Here we find ourselves getting to the heart of the letter, for the church of which Christians are now a part, that strange collection of professing believers who gather together, is a visual aid, a picture of what God has done in the 'heavenly realms'.

WHERE HISTORY IS HEADING

We are told in the first chapter that God has revealed his purposes for history: 'And he made known to us the mystery of his will according to his good pleasure, which he purposed in Christ, to be put into effect when the times will have reached their fulfilment – to bring all things in heaven and earth together under one head, even Christ' (Eph. 1:9, 10).

The end point of history is a church, a group of redeemed people from every nation, tribe, language and tongue, who have been reconciled to God and to one another in Christ, singing his praises for all eternity in a new heaven and new earth. Ephesians teaches us that in some senses this future reality is seen now in the church. Those who have responded to Christ have already been spiritually raised with him to the heavenly realms. There he has authority over all things. He is 'far above all rule and authority, power and dominion and every title that can be given, not only in the present age but also in the one to come.' (1:21); and there we have every spiritual blessing.

It is that new identity which radically affects how we live in the 'earthly realm'. Those who were alienated, which in the context of this letter is the Jew and the Gentile, have been reconciled. A new community has been formed with new values and new relationships, so all-encompassing that the rulers and authorities in the heavenly realms look at the church, this new community, and see the manifold wisdom of God in operation (3:10). Here is something new, something profoundly powerful, affecting our relationship with fellow believers, our relationship with the world and our domestic relationships (between husbands and wives, children and parents, slaves and master).

A CHURCH UNDER FIRE

The church, therefore, in all its wonder, is the present expression of eternity, a demonstration of where history is heading. She has been described by one commentator as 'God's pilot scheme for the reconciled universe of the future.' But as such, the church is under attack. If it is by our love one for another that the world might see we are disciples of Jesus (John 13:34, 35); if the church thereby becomes the most powerful apologetic for the gospel, then it will be the church which finds herself under attack. No wonder it is so difficult to 'be church'. Our battle to be what we are in Christ is not against flesh and blood, but against the rulers, against the authorities, against the powers of this dark world and against the spiritual forces of evil in the heavenly realms.

Satan does not want the church either to be formed (by gospel proclamation) or to live as it should (in gospel ethics). And he does not want the church to live as the church (what we might call 'Gospel living'). And so we need the armour of God, the armour he gives to his Messiah in battle; the armour of Christ. As we put on his armour, as we understand who we are in Christ, so the battle can be won. For Christ has been exalted far above all rule and authority, power and dominion. It is in him that the battle to be the church is won. No wonder Paul is so keen to make it clear that we have every spiritual blessing in Christ and that we have been raised with him. We can be the church and we understand the significance of our identity being in him.

And so Ephesians does have a single theme, from which many implications flow; a theme of what it means to be the church, in Christ, reconciled and raised with him; and what that new community, created in the heavenly realms, should look like in the earthly realm. It is wonderfully heartening to know that the churches of which we are a part and within which we minister are not the irrelevant rumps that society would have us believe, but a profound picture of where history is heading and a living apologetic for the gospel. When we unlock Ephesians we set the church on fire.

THE PRINCIPALITIES AND POWERS

In the light of what we read in the book of Acts, and with the powerful imagery of the warfare in which we are engaged

in Ephesians 6:10-20, it is legitimate to
ask whether Paul had his experiences of
the Artemis cult in Ephesus in mind as he
wrote about the principalities and powers
which fight against the church of Jesus
Christ. Homer – an ancient Greek poet –
is known to have called Artemis 'mistress
of wild beasts', which perhaps explains
Paul's comments in 1 Corinthians 15:32, 'If
I fought wild beasts in Ephesus for merely
human reasons, what have I gained?' But
equally, it is strange how little Paul refers
to principalities and powers in this way in
his subsequent writing.

The opposition in Ephesus clearly
came initially because people were coming to Christ. As those who were previously under the authority of Satan (as in
Eph. 2:1-3) become Christians, a cosmic
and spiritual event was taking place, as
indeed happens whenever people become
Christians. The book of Revelation
reminds us that the beast 'was given

power to make war against the saints and to conquer them, and he was given authority over every tribe, people, language and nation. All inhabitants of the earth will worship the beast – all whose names have not been written in the book of life' (Rev. 13:7, 8). Despite a different background and occasion for writing, this is still written for the church in Ephesus; whose responsibility it is to be witnesses in the world. As the gospel is proclaimed to the world under Satan's authority, so those from every nation, tribe, people and language (7:9) will respond. The enemy is conquered by the proclamation of the gospel (12:11).

In Ephesians the church clearly has that same responsibility as it engages in a fallen world; and to that extent the powers which are confronted by the gospel are those at the command of Satan – powers which can only be overcome by being in Christ. It is also true, as in Revelation, that what threatens the church is the attack of Satan – but what Paul focuses on in order to correct that is not the power of the Artemis cult (a particular manifestation of Satan's warfare), but rather the power of the gospel and the word to bring about true growth in the church. His warnings to the Ephesian elders do not relate to Artemis and to the spiritual power associated with the cult, but rather to false teaching – which is clearly far more likely to do real damage to the church. His instruction to Timothy is to silence false teachers and to instruct the church so that she can be the church. Likewise, within the letter to the Ephesians, Chapter 4 plays a key role in explaining how the word equips Christians to serve so that, as they serve, the church grows to unity and maturity.

Despite the Demetrius-inspired civil revolt, there is no indication in Acts that the church suffered very much from it. The senior civil leaders not only appear to have supported Paul but also to have silenced the rioters. The church was growing beforehand and, as far as we know, it was growing afterwards. There is no report by the elders at Miletus that the Artemis cult was an on-going problem. Paul's real concern was the danger from within the church rather than from without.

As we read the letter it is evident that Satan is the one from whose authority the gospel rescues people. It is also clear that he seeks to attack that which God has made by the gospel; and whilst this is seen in Ephesus through what happened in connection with the Artemis cult, we would not want to view the whole letter through that particular lens and assume that whenever Paul mentions spiritual powers they relate to a pagan experience which will not touch most of us in the 21st century.

3

Every blessing in Christ (1:1-14)

In his commentary on Ephesians, John Stott introduces us to John Mackay, the former president of Princeton Theological Seminary. As a young man his life was turned upside down by reading Paul's letter to the Ephesians, for there he discovered the centrality and magnitude of Christ. 'Jesus Christ became the centre of everything,' he said, 'I had been quickened; I was really alive.' Later, when invited to deliver the Croall Lectures in Edinburgh in 1947, he chose to preach this great letter, referring to it as 'pure music ... what we read here is truth that sings, doctrine set to music.'

Even a cursory reading of the first fourteen verses of the letter will give us some understanding of what Mackay experienced in his own life and later sought to convey in his preaching. These introductory words set the tone for the whole letter. Densely packed with Christian doctrine, they are wide in their portrayal of salvation history and almost poetic in their presentation. They take us on a tour of God's purposes in Christ, from before the foundation of the world to his future inheritance in the new heaven and the new earth. These are words which must first and foremost glorify God.

After his initial introduction, Paul breaks into a wonderful hymn of praise running as one long continual sentence of 202 words from verses 3-14. Certain features can be seen to shape this eulogy.

The focus is clearly the praise of God for his blessings. Verses 3-14 begin with praise: 'Praise be to God' and end with 'to the praise of his glory'. Within these books-ends of praise we see the nature of the work of God from before the foundation of the world to our future inheritance in glory. God's purposes, past, present and future are set out for us.

The spheres in which we experience and enjoy God's blessings are 'in Christ' and 'in the heavenly realms'. All the gifts between verses 3-14 are part of this package of blessing and are therefore grounds for giving praise to God.

The way in which the blessings are experienced is through the agency of the Holy Spirit: the blessings are from God, in Christ, mediated by the Spirit.

In these verses we have the plan and purposes of God unfolded for us. What was hidden has now been made known; the purposes of God in history are no longer a secret. God's purposes in Christ are 'to be put into effect when the times have reached their fulfilment – to bring all things in heaven and on earth together under one head, even Christ' (1:9, 10).

There is also a hint in these verses of what is yet to come in the rest of the letter. As the nature and sphere of God's blessings are explained and his purposes for history are revealed, so also the present outworking of that is now being seen in the church. The end of the eulogy praises God for the emergence of a new community, made up of Jew and Gentile who together share the promise of the future and who will display a picture of that future in their lives together.

(1) Paul, an apostle of Christ Jesus by the will of God, to the saints in Ephesus, the faithful in Christ Jesus: (2) Grace and peace to you from God the Father and the Lord Jesus Christ. (3) Praise be to the God and Father of our Lord Jesus Christ, who has blessed us in the heavenly realms with every spiritual blessing in Christ. (4) For he chose us in him before the creation of the world to be holy and blameless in his sight. In love (5) he predestined us to be adopted as his sons through Jesus Christ, in accordance with his pleasure and will – (6) to the praise of his glorious grace, which he has freely given us in the one he loves. (7) In him we have redemption through his blood, the forgiveness of sins, in accordance with the riches of God's grace, (8) that he lavished on us with all wisdom and understanding. (9) And he made known to us the mystery of his will according to his good pleasure, which he purposed in Christ, (10) to be put into effect when the

times will have reached their fulfilment –
to bring all things in heaven and on earth
together under one head, even Christ.
(11) In him we were chosen, having been
predestined according to the plan of him
who works out everything in conformity
with the purpose of his will, (12) in order that we, who were the first to hope
in Christ, might be for the praise of his
glory. (13) And you also were included
in Christ when you heard the word of
truth, the gospel of your salvation. Having believed, you were marked in him
with a seal, the promised Holy Spirit, (14)
who is a deposit guaranteeing our inheritance until the redemption of those who
are God's possession – to the praise of
his glory.

INTRODUCTIONS (1:1-2)
Although adopting what was no more
than the usual style of greeting for ancient letter writing, Paul begins his letter
with powerful hints as to what the rest of

the letter might contain. The fact that Paul is an apostle not only reminds us that he has been 'sent', but also that he is uniquely qualified to be the bearer of the gospel of Jesus Christ (2:20; 3:5). He is operating as a servant of King Jesus. It is by the will of God that he proclaims this message.

The recipients of the letter are described as 'saints', those who have been made holy and, indeed, as we read the letter, those who are expected and empowered to live increasingly holy lives. In the mixed pagan culture of Ephesus it is their faith, given by God, which enables them to be part of this new community and to live as light in a dark world.

This God-given message which creates this church is mediated by grace and it is by grace that the church which it produces comes about (1:6, 7; 2:5, 7, 8; 3:2, 7, 8; 4:7; 6:24). Likewise the peace which is from 'God our Father and the Lord Jesus Christ' is a peace which is mediated to them in making the church and experienced in them as they live as the church (2:14, 15, 17; 4:3; 6:15, 23).

EVERY SPIRITUAL BLESSING IN CHRIST (1:3)
Here, in this wonderful expression of praise, we are introduced to a term which is both unique to Ephesians and fundamental to it. The 'heavenly realms', or 'heavenlies', appears a number of times (1:3, 20; 2:6; 3:10; 6:12). A cursory reading of the way in which the term is used might initially confuse us. It is the sphere of our blessing (1:3), the place to which Christ has been raised (1:20), the place to which the believer has also been raised spiritually (2:6); the view-point from which the rulers and authorities look at the church (3:10) and the place of spiritual warfare and conquest (6:12).

When we put these verses together we can see that the heavenly realms are where

the principalities and powers are located,
over which the risen Jesus has higher and
total authority not only in the present age
but also in the one to come. He has been
placed there and given all authority, we
are told, for the church (1:20).

We are clearly not yet in the heavenly
realms physically. The Ephesians, like us,
would have known only too well some of
the reality of what life is like in the earthly
realms. Indeed, the letter is written so that
we might increasingly express here what
we have been made there, as we head towards that day when all things, in heaven
and on earth are brought together under
one head, Christ.

PRAISE FOR ELECTION AND ADOPTION (THE
PAST BLESSINGS)(1:4-6)
The nature and benefits of these blessings
now start to be unfolded (the verse begins
with 'even as' or 'for') as we are taken behind
the curtain of history. God's purpose in

making a people finds its origins not in those who choose to become a part of that people, but in his intentions before the foundation of the world. It is all from him.

His purpose and intention for his people is that we would be holy and blameless and loving (see Rom. 8:29). Without the benefits of sentence breaks it can be difficult to know whether 'in love' of v.4 should go with the first part of v.4 (in which case God chose us to be holy, blameless and loving) or the first part of v.5 (in which case God's motive in choosing us was love). However, on balance it seems more likely that Paul meant to make a statement about the people God was creating. Later he will instruct the church to 'live a life of love' modelled on the Lord Jesus – that is what God wants from his people. He is making a people who will present eternity to the world, (a place where the love of people will be perfected as we bask in the glory of the God who is love).

But this new people will not relate to God out of duty but as his children. We are predestined to be adopted as sons. For the Jew, sonship would have been identified with the privileges of Israel (Exod. 4:22; Isa. 1:2; Hosea 11:1). For the Gentile, the Graeco-Roman practice of adoption might have been in mind. Either way, here was something new. This was written to all the saints, the Christians, together – both Jew and Gentile. Now a new people will relate to him as sons, through Christ, because of God's will and pleasure, and therefore inevitably, to the praise of his glorious grace.

As we come to the end of verse 6 and move to verse 7 we see the purposes of God break into the plane of human history. Once again, all is in Christ (in the one he loves) and thoroughly undeserved (he has freely given it).

PRAISE FOR REDEMPTION AND FORGIVENESS (PRESENT BLESSINGS)(1:7-8)

As we enter the stage of human history, the tense of the verbs changes. In the past God had chosen us, predestined us and adopted us. Now, because of Christ we have redemption and forgiveness. These, along with knowledge of the gospel and the down-payment of the Spirit, are present realities for the Christian; and they have been achieved through the blood of Jesus.

All three terms here – blood, redemption and the forgiveness of sins – are loaded with Old Testament meaning but are not fully explained here. Whilst reference is made to the effect of the cross, the mechanism of atonement is not explained. It must be assumed that a) the Ephesian church had sufficient understanding of what Paul meant by these terms and b) that the cross is essential to form the church (Paul does explain the centrality of the cross in 2:14-16) but it is not the main focus of the letter. It may be reasonable to assume that, like many churches today, it is possible for believers to articulate a theology of the cross clearly without grasping its implication for the way in which we relate to each other as the church.

What is unexpected is the phrase 'with all wisdom and understanding'. We do not naturally think that wisdom and understanding relate to redemption and forgiveness, but without a right understanding of the cross we cannot have wisdom and understanding to live as God's people.

PRAISE FOR GOD'S FUTURE PLAN FOR THE WORLD (FUTURE BLESSINGS)(1:9-10)
In the Bible the word 'mystery' is not used of something which cannot be understood, but rather of something which has not been disclosed. Paul tells us that the

mystery, the hidden secret, has been made known: God's will, purposed in Christ, seen in fulness at the end of time, is to bring all things in heaven and on earth under one head, who is Christ.

Here we see the two 'realms' which run as strands throughout this letter, being brought together. We have already been introduced to the heavenly realms in verse 3. Now the earthly realm is introduced, the place in which we now live (see also 1:10; 3:15; 4:9; 6:3). God's purpose in history, that to which all we see and experience is heading, relates to the rule of Christ. The great surprise of this revealed mystery is that God is making a new people, comprised of Jew and Gentile, those who were previously alienated; and that both will share together in the promise of Christ Jesus (3:5, 6).

That may not seem much to us, until we realise just how alienated those two groups were. Chapter 2 will shed more light on the gulf between the two groups and the wonderful grace of God in bringing them together. For now we need to note that the focal point of history is Jesus Christ and a people gathered round him. He is not simply the means of becoming part of this new people; he is our head and our focus.

What should surprise us as we read on is that God has begun this process already, in the earthly realm, as he has brought Jew and Gentile together through the gospel. The Gospel brings the future into the present by the formation of the church.

PRAISE FOR A NEW PEOPLE AND SHARED INHERITANCE (1:11-14)

As we read these verses, which are still part of our long, original sentence, we notice that there is a distinction between the 'we' of verses 11, 12 and the 'you' of verse 13. By the time we come to the end of the section, in verse 14, we discover that the inheritance is 'ours'.

The Jews were always regarded as God's people. The gospel was promised to them, having been announced in advance to Abraham (Gal. 3:8); it was first for them and then for the Gentiles (Rom. 1:16). In the Song of Moses (Deut. 32:8, 9), God's people are referred to as his 'portion' or inheritance. (Hence ESV 1:11 'In him we have obtained an inheritance'). Those Jews who were the first to hope in Christ were the faithful remnant who believed his promises. They were his inheritance; their salvation was to the praise of his glory.

But what is wonderful, and extraordinary, is that through the gospel (the revealed mystery of God), the Gentiles can also be included in this new people as they hear the word of truth and believe (v. 13). And so the glory which goes to God in praise as the Jews become believers in the

Lord Jesus (v. 12) is mirrored as the Gentiles are included (v. 13).

There is now a new people with a new inheritance, hinted at in verses 9-10 and seen worked out in the present reality of the church. The guarantor of that inheritance is the Spirit, given as a deposit of what is yet to come. It is as we are filled with him (the Spirit) that we can live now as new people (see notes on 5:18f), displaying to the principalities the wisdom of God, and to the world the power of the gospel. As we shall discover throughout Ephesians, Gospel power is seen in the formation of the church and in the living of the church. Neither would be possible without the initiative of God, mediated by Christ and experienced through the transforming work of the Spirit.

And so…?

So far, the text has not asked anything of its hearers. There is no command or point

of action. However, this passage is over-
flowing with praise which comes from
a right understanding of what God has
done for us in Christ. That must be our
response too. We long for the response of
praise to God for his overwhelming goodness to us in Christ Jesus. Do we have it?

Here are some clear lessons to help you
praise the God and Father of our Lord
Jesus Christ:

* The church comes about by God's
  initiative.

* We can only understand who we are
  and be who we are by means of the
  cross.

* The church is a picture of the future,
  which we can experience now, in part,
  by the Spirit.

Study Questions

Use these questions on your own, one-to-one with a friend, or in a group to help you get into the book of Ephesians.

Introductory Questions

1. What confidence and expectation do we have as we read the opening verses of Ephesians (1:1-2)? (See also 3:4-6)

2. Describe Jesus according to 1:19-22.

3. How does this relate to the believer? (See 2:6)

4. In the light of this, what does it mean to say that the believer 'has been blessed in the heavenly realms with every spiritual blessing in Christ'? (1:3)

5. How might this affect our thinking and behaviour? (It is helpful to think about how these truths were expected to affect the Ephesians e.g. 4:1, 17, 25-32)

1:3-14 STUDYING THE PASSAGE

1. What has God done for the believer?

2. By what means has he done it?

3. Given what we know about humanity from Ephesians (2:1-3), why is it so important to know that God has chosen us?

4. From our perspective, how do we become a part of what God is doing?

5. From these verses, what does the Christian have in the present?

6. How does this affect our future?

7. How would you explain the difference between what the Christian already has and what is yet to come?

8. Explain why Paul uses 'we', 'you' and 'our' in verses 11-14.

9. In what way have these verses changed your thinking? (About God, Jesus, the Holy Spirit, yourself, the church?)

10. How might this passage change the way you behave this week?

Further Resources

The following books are both targeted and straightforward and will prove useful in getting to grips with Ephesians a little more:

- *Teaching Ephesians* by Simon Austen, published by Christian Focus (2012)

- *The message of Ephesians* by John Stott, published by IVP (1991)

- *Ephesians, an introduction and commentary* by Francis Foulkes published by IVP (1989)

- *Ephesians, the purpose of God* by R.C. Sproul published by Christian Focus (2002)

RESOURCES

TEACHING
EPHESIANS

From text to message

SIMON AUSTEN

SERIES EDITORS: DAVID JACKMAN & ADRIAN REYNOLDS

ISBN 978-1-84550-684-1

Teaching Ephesians

From Text to Message
SIMON AUSTEN

There are commentaries, and there are books on preaching –
but very few books that are specifically geared to the preacher
or Bible teacher tackling a series on a Bible book or doctrinal
theme.

Key features of books in this series are introductory chapters
on 'getting our bearings in the book' and 'planning a series'. The
'meat' of the book then works systematically through a suggested
series, working with the Bible teacher from text to sermon or talk.
Each chapter ends with a suggested preaching/teaching outline
and a detailed Bible study which would be ideal for small groups.

Books in this series are aimed at developing confidence in
handling God's Word in a variety of contexts. Whether you are
a preacher, a small group study leader or youth worker, these
books will give you the necessary tools for teaching. *Teaching
Ephesians* is a welcome addition to the series.

Who are we to be in this materialistic age? Our identity,
Ephesians tells us, can only be found in Christ. The spiritual
blessings that we receive can only be found in Him. We are
chosen and raised in Him. We form together to be the church in
Him. Ephesians paints for us a glorious picture of who we are
and what the church is meant to be as we seek to teach others
with these timeless truths.

Simon Austen has degrees in science and theology. A previous
chaplain of Stowe School, he is now Vicar of Houghton and
Kingmoor in Carlisle, England.

All Titles in the *Teaching* Series...

Teaching 1 Peter
ISBN 978-1-84550-347-5

Teaching 1 Timothy
ISBN 978-1-84550-808-1

Teaching Acts
ISBN 978-1-84550-255-3

Teaching Amos
ISBN 978-1-84550-142-6

Teaching Ephesians
ISBN 978-1-84550-684-1

Teaching Isaiah
ISBN 978-1-84550-565-3

Teaching John
ISBN 978-1-85792-790-0

Teaching Matthew
ISBN 978-1-84550-480-9

Teaching Romans (vol. 1)
ISBN 978-1-84550-455-7

Teaching Romans (vol. 2)
ISBN 978-1-84550-456-4

Teaching the Christian Hope
ISBN 978-1-85792-518-0

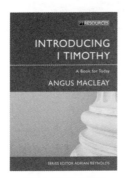

978-1-78191-060-3

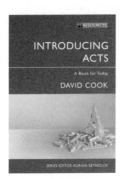

978-1-84550-824-1

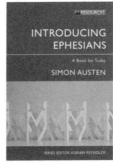

978-1-78191-059-7

Introducing Series

Introducing 1 Timothy
(ANGUS MACLEAY)

Introducing Acts
(DAVID COOK)

Introducing Ephesians
(SIMON AUSTEN)

These are books which will equip you for your own study of Ephesians, 1 Timothy and Acts, ultimately in teaching them. It will help you answer the questions: Why did things happen the way they did? Why should we read these books of the Bible today? What are the main themes? These are Pocket Guide versions of *Teaching 1 Timothy* (978-1-84550-808-1), *Teaching Acts* (978-1-84550-255-3) and *Teaching Ephesians* (978-1-84550-684-1), and each include an introductory study.

David Cook has recently retired from his role as Principal and Director of the School of Preaching at Sydney Missionary and Bible College (SMBC). He is now involved in an itinerant preaching and teaching ministry.

Angus Macleay is the Rector of St. Nicholas, a large Anglican Church in Sevenoaks, and is also a member of the Church of England General Synod.

Simon Austen has degrees in Science and Theology. A previous chaplain of Stowe School, he is now Vicar of Houghton and Kingmoor in Carlisle, England.

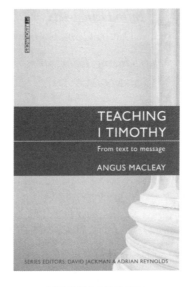

TEACHING
I TIMOTHY

From text to message

ANGUS MACLEAY

SERIES EDITORS, DAVID JACKMAN & ADRIAN REYNOLDS

ISBN 978-1-84550-808-1

Teaching 1 Timothy

From Text to Message

ANGUS MACLEAY

This useful resource, alongside the others in this growing Teaching the Bible Series, is for those who have the privilege and the joy of teaching or preaching a particular book or theme from the Bible. Whether you are a small group leader, preacher or youth worker, it will help you to communicate the message from 1 Timothy. This book will provide a useful launching pad for biblical exposition planning and executing a lesson or sermon in particular with background, structure, key points and application.

Timothy from Lystra was known as 'son' of Paul the apostle who, as his apprentice, was to learn the things of the faith from him. Timothy was later to be sent to Ephesus serving as Paul's representative. The Ephesians had lost their focus on the message of the gospel. They were materialistic and their lives were marked by ungodly living. Timothy's task was to call them back to the cross and what Jesus Christ had done for them, setting their sights on what they will receive when Christ returns for them. Until then they were to live lives of godliness and holiness. This book will help you to teach on 1 Timothy, showing how we can navigate a godly life even in today's culture.

Angus Macleay is the Rector of St Nicholas, a large Anglican church in Sevenoaks, and is also a member of the Church of England General Synod. One of St Nicholas' previous ministers was the poet, John Donne. The recent story of the church is told by the book *The Church that Went Under*. In the 'Teaching the Bible series' Angus MacLeay has also written *Teaching 1 Peter* (ISBN 978-1-84550-347-5).

PROCLAMATION
TRUST MEDIA

TEACHING
JOHN

Unlocking the Gospel of John
for the Bible Teacher

DICK LUCAS & WILLIAM PHILIP

SERIES EDITORS: DAVID JACKMAN & ROBIN SYDSERFF

ISBN 978-1-85792-790-0

Teaching John

Unlocking the Gospel of John for the Bible Teacher

DICK LUCAS AND WILLIAM PHILIP

Preachers find themselves turning to John's Gospel time and time again. This is a primer to explore the main themes of his Gospel. Its purpose is to give the preacher a way into the text that will enable it to be preached in a way that is consonant with its original purpose.

The purpose that John gives for writing his Gospel is found in chapter 20. It is this key that is then used to unlock four very famous chapters in the book.

Many commentaries are written on John but very few take into account the needs of the preacher and congregation combined. This book aims to provide the missing ingredient that will help congregations and preachers come together with the sermon as the point of contact.

Dick Lucas is formerly rector of St Helens Bishopgate, London.

Dr William J. U. Philip is currently minister of St George's Tron Church of Scotland in the city centre of Glasgow. Prior to this, he worked as Director of Ministry for The Proclamation Trust for five years.

TEACHING
ROMANS

Volume One - Unlocking Romans 1-8
for the Bible Teacher

CHRISTOPHER ASH

SERIES EDITORS: DAVID JACKMAN & ROBIN SYDSERFF

ISBN 978-1-84550-455-7

Teaching Romans

Volume 1: Unlocking Romans 1–8 for the Bible Teacher

CHRISTOPHER ASH

There are commentaries and there are books on preaching – but very few books that combine elements of both to enable the preacher or Bible teacher to prepare a series on specific sections of Scripture.

This series gives the Bible teacher suitable tools to understand the context of biblical books; doctrinal themes; the methods of interpretation; the key interpretation points and how to communicate that message for the hearer. Whilst very useful for preachers, this book is also aimed at equipping small group study leaders, youth workers and other Bible teachers.

The books are purposefully practical. Section One contains 'navigation' material to get you into the text of Romans. Section Two works systematically through a suggested preaching or Bible study series. Preaching outlines and Bible study questions are included for each passage.

Christopher Ash is an ordained minister in the Anglican Church and Director of the Cornhill Training Course, a one-year course designed to provide Bible-handling and practical ministry skills to those exploring their future role in Christian work.

TEACHING
ROMANS

Volume Two - Unlocking Romans 9-16
for the Bible Teacher

CHRISTOPHER ASH

SERIES EDITORS: DAVID JACKMAN & ROBIN SYDSERFF

ISBN 978-1-84550-456-4

Teaching Romans

Volume 2: Unlocking Romans 9–16 for the Bible Teacher

CHRISTOPHER ASH

There are commentaries and there are books on preaching – but very few books that combine elements of both to enable the preacher or Bible teacher to prepare a series on specific sections of Scripture.

This series gives the Bible teacher suitable tools to understand the context of biblical books; doctrinal themes; the methods of interpretation; the key interpretation points and how to communicate that message for the hearer. Whilst very useful for preachers, this book is also aimed at equipping small group study leaders, youth workers and other Bible teachers.

The books are purposefully practical. Section One contains 'navigation' material to get you into the text of Romans. Section Two works systematically through a suggested preaching or Bible study series. Preaching outlines and Bible study questions are included for each passage.

Christopher Ash is an ordained minister in the Anglican Church and Director of the Cornhill Training Course, a one-year course designed to provide Bible-handling and practical ministry skills to those exploring their future role in Christian work.

PT Resources

www.proctrust.org.uk
Resources for preachers and Bible teachers

PT Resources, a ministry of The Proclamation Trust, provides a range of multimedia resources for preachers and Bible teachers.

Books

The *Teaching the Bible* series, published jointly with *Christian Focus Publications*, is written by preachers, for preachers, and is specifically geared to the purpose of God's Word – its proclamation as living truth. Books in the series aim to help the reader move beyond simply understanding a text to communicating and applying it.

Current titles include: *Teaching 1 Peter*, *Teaching 1 Timothy*, *Teaching Acts*, *Teaching Amos*, *Teaching Ephesians*, *Teaching Isaiah*, *Teaching Matthew*, *Teaching Romans*, and *Teaching the Christian Hope*.

Forthcoming titles include: *Teaching Daniel, Teaching Mark, Teaching Numbers, Teaching Nehemiah* and *Teaching 1&2 Samuel*.

DVD TRAINING

Preaching & Teaching the Old Testament: 4 DVDs – Narrative, Prophecy, Poetry, Wisdom

Preaching & Teaching the New Testament 3 DVDs – Gospels, Letters, Acts & Revelation

These training DVDs aim to give preachers and teachers confidence in handling the rich variety of God's Word. David Jackman has taught this material to generations of Cornhill students, and gives us step-by-step instructions on handling each genre of biblical literature.

He demonstrates principles that will guide us through the challenges of teaching and applying different parts of the Bible, for example:

- How does prophecy relate to the lives of its hearers – ancient and modern?
- How can you preach in a way that reflects the deep emotion of the psalms?

Both sets are suitable for preachers and for those teaching the Bible in a wide variety of contexts.

- Designed for **individual** and **group** study
- Interactive learning through many **worked examples** and **exercises**
- Flexible format ideal for **training courses**
- Optional **English subtitles** for second-language users
- Print as many **workbooks** as you need (PDF)

AUDIO

PT Resources has a large range of Mp3 downloads, nearly all of which are entirely free to download and use.

PREACHING INSTRUCTION

This series aims to help the preacher or teacher understand, open up and teach individual books of the Bible by getting to grips with their central message and purpose.

SERMON SERIES

These sermons, examples of great preaching, not only demonstrate faithful biblical preaching but will also refresh and instruct the hearer.

CONFERENCES

Recordings of our conferences include challenging topical addresses, discussion of preaching and ministry issues, and warm-hearted exposition that will challenge and inspire all those in ministry.

Christian Focus Publications

publishes books for all ages

Our mission statement –

STAYING FAITHFUL

In dependence upon God we seek to impact the world through literature faithful to His infallible Word, the Bible. Our aim is to ensure that the LORD Jesus Christ is presented as the only hope to obtain forgiveness of sin, live a useful life and look forward to heaven with Him.

REACHING OUT

Christ's last command requires us to reach out to our world with His gospel. We seek to help fulfil that by publishing books that point people towards Jesus and help them develop a Christ-like maturity. We aim to equip all levels of readers for life, work, ministry and mission.

Books in our adult range are published in three imprints:

Christian Focus contains popular works including biographies, commentaries, basic doctrine and Christian living. Our children's books are also published in this imprint.

Mentor focuses on books written at a level suitable for Bible College and seminary students, pastors, and other serious readers. The imprint includes commentaries, doctrinal studies, examination of current issues and church history.

Christian Heritage contains classic writings from the past.

Christian Focus Publications Ltd
Geanies House, Fearn,
Ross-shire, IV20 1TW, Scotland, United Kingdom
info@christianfocus.com

Our titles are available from quality bookstores and
www.christianfocus.com